WHY DO PEOPLE SMOKE ?

Designed and produced by
Aladdin Books Ltd, 70 Old Compton Street, London W1V 5PA

Editor: Catherine Bradley
Design: Rob Hillier, Andy Wilkinson
Picture Research: Cecilia Weston-Baker
Illustration: Ron Hayward Associates
Consultant: Angela Grunsell

Pete Sanders is a head teacher of a London elementary
school and is working with groups of teachers on
personal, social and health education. Angela Grunsell
is an advisory teacher specializing in development
education and resources for the primary school age
range.

The publishers would like to thank all the children and
adults who posed for the photographs in this book.

Published in the United States in 1989 by
Gloucester Press, 387 Park Avenue South, New York, NY 10016

Printed in Belgium   All rights reserved

ISBN 0-531-17192-2

Library of Congress Catalog
Card Number: 89-50449

"LET'S TALK ABOUT"

WHY DO PEOPLE SMOKE ?

PETE SANDERS

Gloucester Press
New York · London · Toronto · Sydney

"What does smoking have to do with me?"

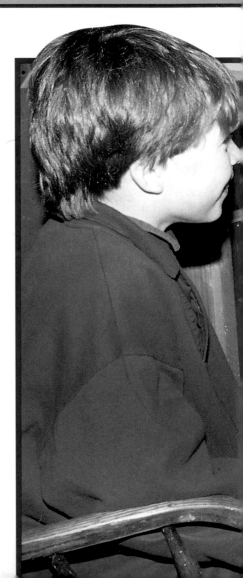

We live in a world where people are allowed to smoke. You might know somebody who does. About one in every three people smoke. Many of these smokers say that they didn't mean to carry on doing it. It's likely that they didn't care for the taste when they tried their first cigarettes. They made a choice to get used to smoking.

As you grow up, you have the chance to make your own choices about what you do. Knowing what choices there are, and what the results might be can help you to decide. Often there can be so many reasons for coming to a particular decision. For example, you might do something to look good to other people. You might say that somebody else made you do something. Although this might sometimes be true, it isn't always the case. People can forget that they can please themselves. There is no need to copy a bad habit that a friend or a member of your family may have.

4

Talking things over with your friends often helps you to decide what might be the best thing to do.

"What are cigarettes?"

Cigarettes are made from the leaves of the tobacco plant. People have been smoking tobacco for hundreds of years. The leaves have to be dried and mixed with chemicals to help them stay moist. Then they are wrapped in paper. When the cigarette is lit, the tobacco burns. As it does, all the different substances in the tobacco are breathed into the body. There are at least a thousand substances, and many of them are known to be harmful, for example, ammonia, carbon monoxide and tar. The tobacco leaves also contain nicotine. This is a drug. Many smokers find their bodies are so used to the nicotine, that it is difficult for them to do without it. This is one of the reasons they carry on smoking.

> Most people smoke tobacco as cigarettes. Some people chew it, or smoke it in pipes or as cigars.

7

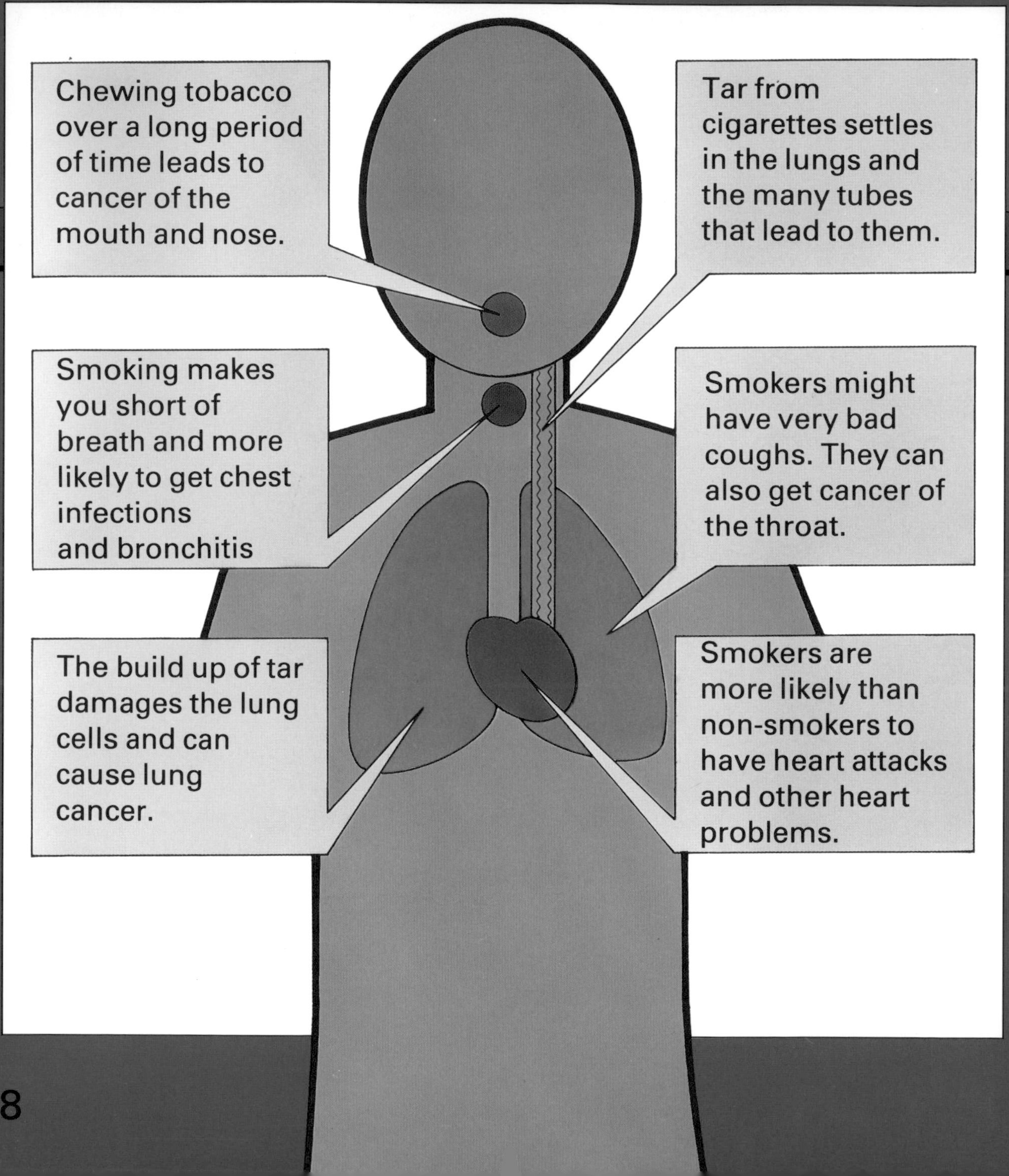
Chewing tobacco over a long period of time leads to cancer of the mouth and nose.
Tar from cigarettes settles in the lungs and the many tubes that lead to them.
Smoking makes you short of breath and more likely to get chest infections and bronchitis
Smokers might have very bad coughs. They can also get cancer of the throat.
The build up of tar damages the lung cells and can cause lung cancer.
Smokers are more likely than non-smokers to have heart attacks and other heart problems.

"How can cigarettes damage your health?"

The body is made up of lots of cells. They all need oxygen. You get this from the air that you breathe into the lungs. Oxygen is then sent around the body through the blood. If people smoke regularly some of the substances in smoke can stop the lungs from doing their job. The tar from cigarettes settles in the lungs and the many tubes that lead to them. This often causes the sore throats and hacking coughs that many smokers suffer from. The tar can also attack the cells. This can lead to cancer, where the cells are out of control and keep growing. Cancer is often fatal.

Carbon monoxide in cigarettes makes it more difficult for blood to carry the oxygen around the body. It can travel around the body along with the blood. This, along with the nicotine, can make the blood much thicker. In some cases, it can get so dense that the flow of blood can stop altogether.

This is what leads to heart attacks.

"Are there other risks when you smoke cigarettes?"

Many fires in the home are caused by cigarettes. Smoking is not allowed in many subways and buses because burning cigarettes have lead to fires. Lots of forest fires are caused by someone carelessly dropping a cigarette that has not been put out completely.

Breathing in air which contains smoke from other peoples' cigarettes is called passive smoking. Non-smokers can get headaches, sore eyes, blocked up or runny noses, coughs and general "stuffed up" feelings. Some people who have asthma find that they become ill. It seems that people who live with smokers are more at risk than those who don't of getting the illnesses that smokers have.

Cigarette smoke can make offices, public places and homes become dirtier more quickly. Some people complain about the cost of cleaning that this causes. They want more and more no-smoking areas.

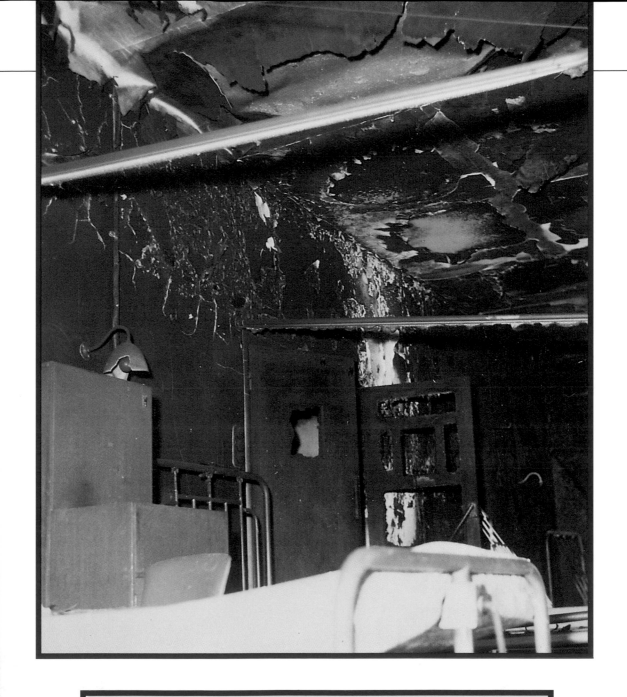

Some fires in the home are started when people fall asleep while smoking in bed.

"Why don't they ban smoking?"

You may be wondering why smoking hasn't been banned. Certainly there are people who want this to happen. But others feel that people would still find ways of getting tobacco in some form and they would break the law to do it. There are also those who say that they have the right to choose.

Some countries try to stop people from smoking by putting warnings about the dangers on the packs, and through anti-smoking advertisements and teaching in schools. At the same time, some governments have passed laws which limit cigarette advertising. For example, they stop commercials from appearing on television.

Cigarette companies can get their products shown on television by sponsoring sporting events. In the United States the tobacco companies spend around fifty times more on advertising than the government does on warning of the risks of smoking.

Cigarette companies make sure their names appear on the sports cars they sponsor.

PRODUCING COUNTRIES

The people who grow tobacco make money out of selling it to the tobacco companies.

TOBACCO COMPANIES

make a lot of money out of cigarettes and employ people making and distributing them.

STORE SALES AND ADVERTISING

People also make money out of selling cigarettes either in stores or through making and selling advertising. If everyone stopped smoking then a lot of people would lose their jobs.

MONEY FOR HEALTH CARE

Every year the government has to spend money paying for people who are ill from smoking.

TAXES TO THE GOVERNMENT

A high percentage of the price of a cigarette pack is taken by the government

"Who gains from cigarette smoking?"

There's a lot of money involved in the sale of cigarettes. Lots of people worldwide have jobs because of cigarettes. The tobacco companies use the countries in Africa, Asia, and South America to grow tobacco. It is cheaper to grow tobacco there. One reason for this is that they don't have to pay the workers very much. People grow tobacco because they want the jobs. You might think that the local people could just change from growing tobacco to other crops. But this would take time and money to do.

In recent years the number of people smoking cigarettes in the United States and Europe has fallen. This means that some people – both growers and factory workers – have lost their jobs. The tobacco companies are turning to countries in Africa, Asia, and South America where they think that they can make money by selling tobacco. Many people feel that this is wrong and should be stopped.

Children who start smoking very young have not always thought about the risks.

"Why do people start smoking?"

People begin to smoke for many different reasons. Some start because they are curious to find out what smoking is like. Other people start smoking because they know it's something that people disapprove of. It makes them feel different from everyone else. Then there are those who want to join in if their friends are smoking. It can be difficult and embarrassing to say no when someone offers them a cigarette. Many of the children who start smoking do so because their parents or friends are doing it.

At times you may have wanted to look more grown up or big in front of your friends. This is the reason that some start to smoke. They don't realize that most adults don't smoke.

In most cases people start smoking because they don't realize that the nicotine in the cigarettes can be hard to give up. This is why it's not a good idea to try a cigarette even if you are curious.

"Why do people smoke?"

The first cigarette most people smoke tastes very unpleasant. After all, breathing smoke into the lungs isn't a natural thing to do. After a few cigarettes people become used to the burning feeling in the back of the throat. Smokers say they like the taste and smell. Some insist that it makes them feel more relaxed. Often, they might explain that they enjoy the ritual of having a cigarette at certain times, like with a cup of coffee, or after a meal or when they are talking on the telephone. Then there are those who believe it helps them to feel more confident. Perhaps they like the feel of a cigarette in their hands.

It appears that a little nicotine in the body can make people more alert and wide awake. People who smoke may just do it out of habit. Most smokers light up without thinking about it. Some smokers like the feel of sucking at a cigarette. It may remind them of a dummy they used when they were little.

Offering cigarettes to others can make people smoke more because they feel they have to offer them back.

Tobacco companies
make special brands
of cigarettes to
appeal to women.

"Does smoking affect people in different ways?"

Researchers are finding that more and more young women are taking up smoking, and that men are giving it up. They are also saying that women find it harder to stop. Why should this be so? Some say it is because women are under pressure. More and more women are working and looking after families, and they may find smoking helps them to cope. Others suggest that girls take up smoking to look more independent.

Whatever the reasons, illnesses caused by smoking are increasing among women. One special concern is for women who are expecting babies. When she is pregnant, the mother shares her blood with the baby, and this helps it to grow inside her. If a pregnant woman smokes, the nicotine and carbon monoxide pass into the bloodstream of the unborn child. This can cause a miscarriage. The babies born to women who smoke often weigh less than other babies.

"Why don't people just stop smoking?"

If you have ever asked any smoker why they carry on doing it, you may have been told that smoking helps them to cope with stress. If there are too many things happening in their lives or they are in a situation where they feel that they have little or no control, they may say that they are unable to cope. Somehow, having a cigarette acts as a comfort for them in these situations.

You may know somebody who gave up smoking and yet started again during a difficult time. It is when people feel that other things are controlling them rather than the other way around that they are likely to smoke again.

Yet, there are other ways that they might cope with the stresses of life. Probably the best one is to talk with others. Some people think about what they are doing and decide to lead a healthier lifestyle. They might plan to eat better, or take up a sport or learn ways of relaxing.

Smoking one cigarette
after another is no way to
cope with stress.

"How difficult is it to give up smoking?"

It can be very difficult for people to give up smoking, even if they want to. It's a hard habit to break. Nicotine is a very powerful drug. When a person quits, it takes time for the body to do without such a drug. During this period, ex-smokers can feel awful. They may get headaches and feel irritable. They can even lose their ability to concentrate. You can see why some people find it very hard to give up.

There are many ways of giving up. Some people stop all at once. Others cut down gradually. Some take something which makes cigarettes taste horrible if they smoke one, or chew gum which contains nicotine. Some try hypnosis or acupuncture.

Some people join support groups. They meet on a regular basis with others who are trying to quit.

"Why don't they have laws to restrict smoking?"

Many people would like there to be new laws to do this. You might think it would be a good idea to ban it altogether. After all, the cost of looking after poeple who are ill from smoking is very high. At the moment, this doesn't seem likely to happen. The government is not going to do that because many smokers would consider it an infringement of their rights, and the government would lose their votes. The government also needs the money it gets from cigarette taxes. If the tobacco companies closed down there would be more unemployed people. These people might not vote for the government either. Another problem for the government is that the tobacco companies have a lot of power and influence.

It's against the law to sell cigarettes to anyone under 16, but many storekeepers do so.

Some restaurants do not allow their customers to smoke because it offends non-smokers.

"What can be done about smoking?"

There are more and more places where it isn't OK to smoke. Many restaurants have areas where people can't smoke, and smoking is not allowed in many movie theaters. Lots of offices and factories have stopped permitting people to smoke in them, or have set aside special rooms for smokers. Some people are upset by this, and they have set up organizations which campaign for smokers' rights.

Some well-known people like pop stars and television personalities do not smoke because they know that others might copy their behavior. Television programs try not to show people smoking as much as they used to.

Since most people start smoking when they are young it makes sense that schools teach children about smoking. You may have learned about it at school or taken part in competitions on national no-smoking day. These are some of the ways that people hope to get you to think about cigarette smoking.

30

"What can I do about smoking?"

Knowing what smoking can do to our bodies can help us to make a decision about whether to smoke or not. Yet even with all the facts, it is interesting that many people choose to accept what they want to believe and not accept what they don't believe. You often feel that nasty things won't happen to you. In any case, it is difficult to understand that it is thought each time you smoke a cigarette you may be taking five minutes off your life.

It's also hard to think so far into the future. People don't usually get seriously ill from smoking until much later in life. But the habits that we start now might have an effect later on. Most smokers say that they wish that they had never started. That is why it's not a particularly good idea to nag smokers to give up. Most people who smoke know that they should not be doing it. Having someone telling them this will not necessarily help them to change.

Index

Photographic credits:

Cover and pages 5, 7, 11, 16, 20, 23, 24, 27 and 29: Marie-Helene Bradley; page 13: Rex Features; page 14 both: Network Photographers; page 19; Vanessa Bailey.

PRINTED IN BELGIUM BY proost INTERNATIONAL BOOK PRODUCTION